Welcome to a compilation of Stories, Quotes, Inspirations and Tips for your morning relaxation or any time you feel the need to just get away in your mind!

All quotes and stories are credited to their authors where the information is available. If we missed crediting something that you know belongs to a particular author, please let us know so that we can correct it. Thank you.

If you have stories or quotes to share for future editions, please email us so they may be considered. Thank you.

By
Dr. Jane F. Cundy
The Business Connection Services
6024 Whisperwood CT NE
Albuquerque, NM 87109
E-mail: info@thebusinessconnection.com

To receive your free copy of "Your Coffee Break for the Brain" newsletter, please email the address listed.

© 2012. All rights reserved.

ISBN: 978-0-9887414-0-9

"Coffee Break for the Brain" newsletters are the original copyrighted work of Dr. Jane Cundy, The Business Connection and The Business Connection Services. The Phrase "Your Coffee Break for the Brain," "Coffee Break for the Brain," and "Remember to Be Kind to Yourself" are ® to Dr. Jane F. Cundy and The Business Connection Services

Introduction

I love collecting quotes and stories from different people and on many different subjects. It started out as a collection just for my enjoyment and then expanded for my weekly newsletter that I send out to clients and interested persons every Monday. I have been sending out my *"Your Coffee Break for the Brain"* news tips and inspirations to business clients and interested persons internationally and over the Southwest and Northwest regions of our country since 2008.

Some of these were so popular that I received a request for me to write an article that was published for a magazine in South Africa! The article was printed in CEO Magazine in April, 2009.

Most of these quotes and stories you can find and read on my website, but I have chosen to make a little book that you can, in the comfort of your own time and space, read just for pleasure; or perhaps there is a quote or story from someone that will assist you in making a decision, taking a chance or making a difference in your life or in the life of someone you love. If this is the case, then the choice to put this together is worth every minute.

I think one of my favorite quotes is on the cover of this book. It always reminds me that the little things that we do or say always make a difference in the lives of others.

As a child my parents used to say *"sticks and stones make break you bones, but words can never hurt you."* Many of us grew up with that belief system in the late fifties and during the sixties, now we know that words make a huge difference.

We remember easily and effortlessly what others have said about us; even if it was years ago and we were in grade school.

There are two problems with this. One is that what we tend to remember are the hurtful words and comments, not the words of praise and comfort provided by those who really do matter. The other problem is that what we remember is distorted by emotions and not the actual words someone said. Why? Because our brain distorts memories and after twenty-four hours what we heard and what we remember are not the same. We tend to exaggerate the memory and over time and it becomes like the gossip told around a circle; by the time it returns to you the story is not even close to what was originally said. If this happens in a room with a group of people and in the same time frame; imagine the story after days, weeks, or even years of holding on to what you thought was true!

Yesterday I was reading stories that I have collected over time and this one, "When You Though I Wasn't Looking," struck me as a good place to begin.

Many of us have children or have family members who have children. If not, I can promise that all of us have been children; some may still be!

I trust that you will find humor, love and wisdom throughout the pages of this book. It is with these thoughts and wishes in mind that I have compiled the stories and quotes, inspirations and tips that I have collected over the years along with news tips and inspirations from my newsletters.

Please note that where possible I have credited the author, when it is not available or it is unknown, I have mentioned that as well.

Enjoy and as always;

"Remember to Be Kind to Yourself!"

Dr Jane F. Cundy

My Thanks and Gratitude
to my dear friend
Casey for
giving me the idea
to do this little book
along with
cheering me on.
Thanks also for being
my great friend,
and supporting me
in all areas of my life.

Stories
That I Have
Collected
Over the Years

WHEN YOU THOUGHT I WASN'T LOOKING
~Author unknown

When you thought I wasn't looking I saw you hang my first painting on the refrigerator, and I immediately wanted to paint another one.

~

When you thought I wasn't looking I saw you feed a stray cat, and I learned that it was good to be kind to animals.

~

When you thought I wasn't looking I saw you make my favorite cake for me, and I learned that the little things can be the special things in life.

~

When you thought I wasn't looking I saw you make a meal and take it to a friend who was sick, and I learned that we all have to help take care of each other.

~

When you thought I wasn't looking, I saw you give of your time and money to help people who had nothing, and I learned that those who have something should give to those who don't.

~

When you thought I wasn't looking I saw you take care of our house and everyone in it, and I learned we have to take care of what we are given.

~

When you thought I wasn't looking I saw how you handled your responsibilities, even when you didn't feel good, and I learned that I would have to be responsible when I grow up.

~

When you thought I wasn't looking I saw tears come from your eyes, and I learned that sometimes things hurt, but it's all right to cry.

~

When you thought I wasn't looking I saw that you cared, and I wanted to be everything that I could be.

~

When you thought I wasn't looking, I learned most of lives lessons that I need to know to be a good and productive person when I grow up.

~

When you thought I wasn't looking, I looked at you and wanted to say, 'Thanks for all the things I saw when you thought I wasn't looking.'

Coins in a Jar
~Author unknown

A little girl went to her bedroom and pulled a glass jelly jar from its hiding place in the closet. She poured the change out on the floor and counted it carefully. Three times, even. The total had to be exactly perfect. No chance here for mistakes.

Carefully placing the coins back in the jar and twisting on the cap, she slipped out the back door and made her way 6 blocks to Rexall's Drug Store with the big Red Indian Chief sign above the door.

She waited patiently for the pharmacist to give her some attention, but he was too busy at this moment.

Tess twisted her feet to make a scuffing noise. Nothing; she cleared her throat with the most disgusting sound she could muster. No good. Finally she took a quarter from her jar and banged it on the glass counter. That did it!

'And what do you want?' the pharmacist asked in an annoyed tone of voice... I'm talking to my brother from Chicago whom I haven't seen in ages,' he said without waiting for a reply to his question.

'Well, I want to talk to you about my brother,' Tess answered back in the same annoyed tone. 'He's really; really sick....and I want to buy a miracle.'

'I beg your pardon?' said the pharmacist.

'His name is Andrew and he has something bad growing inside his head and my Daddy says only a miracle can save him now. So how much does a miracle cost?'

'We don't sell miracles here, little girl. I'm sorry but I can't help you,' the pharmacist said, softening a little.

'Listen, I have the money to pay for it. If it isn't enough, I will get the rest. Just tell me how much it costs.'

The pharmacist's brother was a well dressed man. He stooped down and asked the little girl, 'What kind of a miracle does your brother need?'

'I don't know,' Tess replied with her eyes welling up. I just know he's really sick and Mommy says he needs an operation. But my Daddy can't pay for it, so I want to use my money.'

'How much do you have?' asked the man from Chicago. 'One dollar and eleven cents,' Tess answered barely audible. 'And it's all the money I have, but I can get some more if I need to.'

'Well, what a coincidence,' smiled the man; 'a dollar and eleven cents...the exact price of a miracle for little brothers.'

He took her money in one hand and with the other hand he grasped her mitten and said 'Take me to where you live. I want to see your brother and meet your parents. Let's see if I have the miracle you need.'

That well-dressed man was Dr. Carlton Armstrong, a surgeon, specializing in neuro-surgery. The operation was completed free of charge and it wasn't long until Andrew was home again and doing well.

Mom and Dad were happily talking about the chain of events that had led them to this place.

'That surgery,' her Mom whispered, 'was a real miracle. I wonder how much it would have cost.'

Tess smiled. She knew exactly how much a miracle cost....one dollar and eleven cents...plus the faith of a little child.

Giving Is Receiving
~Marrinel Harriman

"I learned about giving in the slow human way. Because my mother was a skilled nurse to a less fortunate little girl, who lived with disabled parents. After thanking me gratefully, the little girl offered me the only party dress in her closet. Puzzled, I tried to refuse, but my mother guided me. She complimented the girl and told her how happy I would be to wear the dress. I came away knowing a little bit more about human pride and who gives what to whom. My greatest gift to the girl was acceptance of the gift she offered me.

Many years later, I stood by helplessly as our small rabbit Ashley lay dying. The antibiotics no longer worked. Suddenly she noticed a scratch on the shoulder of her friend Lillian. With a last burst of energy she raised her head and began to frantically clean Lillian's sore. Her mission must be accomplished! With more strength than she had summoned in several weeks, she compulsively tended to Lillian's comfort. Lillian's last gift to her dying friend was to receive. Lillian was there to accept Ashley's fond and fervent cleaning.

Several times since then, I have witnessed the same phenomenon. Dying rabbits take care of the attending rabbits, who give by allowing themselves to be cared for. I'm astounded to see animals show such pride, dignity, and a sense of when to give and when to receive.

We--intelligent sophisticated beings that we are--have to learn these things. Our animal friends already know them on their own."

Just a Dog
~Author unknown

"From time to time people tell me, "Lighten up, it's just a dog," or "That's a lot of money for "just a dog." They don't understand the distance traveled, time spent, or costs involved for "Just a dog." Some of my proudest moments have come about with "Just a dog." Many hours have passed with my only company being "Just a dog, and not once have I felt slighted. Some of my saddest moments were brought about by "Just a dog." In those days of darkness, the gentle touch of "Just a dog" provided comfort and purpose to overcome the day.

"If you, too, think its "Just a dog," you will probably understand phrases like "Just a friend," "Just a sunrise," or "Just a promise." "Just a dog" brings into my life the very essence of friendship, trust, and pure unbridled joy. "Just a dog" brings out the compassion and patience that makes me a better person. Because of "Just a dog" I will rise early, take long walks and look longingly into the future.

For me and folks like me, it's not "Just a dog." It's the thing that gives me humanity and keeps me from being "Just a man or woman."

So, the next time you hear the phrase "Just a dog," smile, because they "Just Don't Understand."

Puppy Size
~Author unknown

Danielle keeps repeating it over and over again. We've been back to this animal shelter at least five times. It has been weeks now since we started all of this," the mother told the volunteer.

"What is it she keeps asking for?" the volunteer asked.

"Puppy size!" replied the mother. "

Well, we have plenty of puppies, if that's what she's looking for."

"I know...we have seen most of them," the mom said in frustration...Just then Danielle came walking into the office. "Well, did you find one?" asked her mom.

"No, not this time," Danielle said with sadness in her voice. "Can we come back on the weekend?"

The two women looked at each other, shook their heads and laughed. "You never know when we will get more dogs. Unfortunately, there's always a supply," the volunteer said.

Danielle took her mother by the hand and headed to the door. "Don't worry, I'll find one this weekend," she said.

Over the next few days both mom and dad had long conversations with her. They both felt she was being too particular."It's this weekend or we're not looking anymore," Dad finally said in frustration.

"We don't want to hear anything more about puppy size either," Mom added.

Sure enough, they were the first ones in the shelter on Saturday morning. By now Danielle knew her way around, so she ran right for the section that housed the smaller dogs.

Tired of the routine, mom sat in the small waiting room at the end of the first row of cages. There was an observation window so you could see the animals during times when visitors weren't permitted.

Danielle walked slowly from cage to cage, kneeling periodically to take a closer look. One by one the dogs were brought out and she held each one. One by one she said, "Sorry, you're not the one."

It was the last cage on this last day in search of the perfect pup. The volunteer opened the cage door and the child carefully picked up the dog and held it closely. This time she took a little longer. "Mom, that's it!

I found the right puppy! He's the one! I know it!" she screamed with joy. "It's the puppy size!"

"But it's the same size as all the other puppies you held over the last few weeks," Mom said.

"No not size ---- the sighs. When I held him in my arms, he sighed," she said.

"Don't you remember? When I asked you one day what love is, you told me love depends on the sighs of your heart. The more you love, the bigger the sigh!"

The two women looked at each other for a moment. Mom didn't know whether to laugh or cry. As she stooped down to hug the child, she did a little of both.

"Mom, every time you hold me, I sigh. When you and Daddy come home from work and hug each other, you both sigh. I knew I would find the right puppy if it sighed when I held it in my arms," she said. Then holding the puppy up close to her face she said, "Mom, he loves me. I heard the sighs of his heart!"

"Until one has loved an animal, a part of one's soul remains unawakened" ~Anatole France

The 'Middle Wife
~By an Anonymous 2nd grade teacher

"I've been teaching now for about fifteen years. I have two kids myself, but the best birth story I know is the one I saw in my own second grade classroom a few years back. When I was a kid, I loved show-and-tell. So I always have a few sessions with my students. It helps them get over shyness and usually, show-and-tell is pretty tame. Kids bring in pet turtles, model airplanes, pictures of fish they catch, stuff like that. And I never, ever place any boundaries or limitations on them. If they want to lug it in to school and talk about it, they're welcome. Well, one day this little girl, Erica, a very bright, very outgoing kid, takes her turn and waddles up to the front of the class with a pillow stuffed under her sweater. She holds up a snapshot of an infant.

'This is Luke, my baby brother, and I'm going to tell you about his birthday...' 'First, Mom and Dad made him as a symbol of their love, and then Dad put a seed in my Mom's stomach, and Luke grew in there. He ate for nine months through an umbrella cord.'

She's standing there with her hands on the pillow, and I'm trying not to laugh and wishing I had my camcorder with me. The kids are watching her in amazement.

'Then, about two Saturdays ago, my Mom starts saying and going, 'Oh, Oh, Oh, Oh!' Erica puts a hand behind her back and groans. 'She walked around the house for, like an hour, 'Oh, oh, oh!' (Now this kid is doing a hysterical duck walk and groaning.)

'My Dad called the middle wife. She delivers babies, but she doesn't have a sign on the car like the Domino's man. They got my Mom to lie down in bed like this.

(Then Erica lies down with her back against the wall.)

And then, pop! My Mom had this bag of water she kept in there in case he got thirsty, and it just blew up and spilled all over the bed, like psshhheew!'

(This kid has her legs spread with her little hands miming water flowing away. It was too much!)

Then the middle wife starts saying 'push, push,' and 'breathe, breathe. They started counting, but never even got past ten. Then, all of a sudden, out comes my brother. He was covered in yucky stuff that they all said it was from Mom's play- center, so there must be a lot of toys inside there.' Then Erica stood up, took a big theatrical bow and returned to her seat.

I'm sure I applauded the loudest.

Ever since then, when it's show-and-tell day, I bring my camcorder, just in case another 'Middle Wife' comes along."

Retarded Grandparents
This was actually reported by a teacher

After Christmas, a teacher asked her young pupils how they spent their holiday away from school. One child wrote the following:

"We always used to spend the holidays with Grandma and Grandpa. They used to live in a big brick house but Grandpa got retarded and they moved to Florida; now they live in a tin box and have rocks painted green to look like grass. They ride around on their bicycles and wear name tags because they don't know who they are anymore.

They go to a building called a wreck center, but they must have got it fixed because it is all okay now, they do exercises there, but they don't do them very well. There is a swimming pool too, but they all jump up and down in it with hats on.

At their gate, there is a doll house with a little old man sitting in it. He watches all day so nobody can escape. Sometimes they sneak out, and go cruising in their golf carts. Nobody there cooks, they just eat out. And they eat the same thing every night --- early birds. Some of the people can't get out past the man in the doll house. The ones who do get out bring food back to the wrecked center for pot luck.

My Grandma says that Grandpa worked all his life to earn his retardment and says I should work hard so I can be retarded someday too. When I earn my retardment, I want to be the man in the doll house. Then I will let people out, so they can visit their grandchildren."

A group of professionals posed this question to a group of 4 to 8 year olds:

What does love mean? The answers they got were broader and deeper than anyone could have imagined.

1. When my grandma got arthritis, she couldn't bend over and paint her toenails anymore; so my grandpa does it for her now all the time, even when his hands got arthritis too. That's love. Rebecca - age 8

2. When someone loves you, the way they say your name is different. You just know that your name is safe in their mouths. Billy - age 4

3. Love is when a girl puts on perfume and a boy puts on shaving cologne and they go out and smell each other. Kari - age 5

4. Love is when you go out to eat and give somebody most of your French fries without making them give you any of theirs. Chrissy - age 6

5. Love is what makes you smile when you're tired. Terri - age 4

6. Love is when my mommy makes coffee for my daddy and she takes a sip before giving it to him, to make sure the taste is OK. Danny - age 7

7. Love is when you kiss all the time. Then when you get tired of kissing, you still want to be together and you talk more. My mommy and my daddy are like that. They look gross when they kiss. Emily – age 8

8. Love is what's in the room with you at Christmas if you stop opening presents and listen. Bobby - age 7

9. If you want to learn to love better, you should start with a friend who you hate. Nikka - age 6

10. Love is when you tell a guy you like his shirt, then he wears it every day. Noelle - age 7

11. Love is like a little old woman and a little old man who are still friends even after they know each other so well. Tommy - age 6

12. During my piano recital, I was on stage and I was scared. I looked at all the people watching me and saw my daddy waving and smiling. He was the only one doing that. I wasn't scared anymore. Cindy - age 8

13. My mommy loves me more than anybody. You don't see anyone else kissing me to sleep at night. Clare - age 6

14. Love is when mommy gives daddy the best piece of chicken. Elaine - age 5

15. Love is when mommy sees daddy smelly and sweaty and still says he is handsomer than Robert Redford. Chris - age 7

16. Love is when your puppy licks your face even after you left him alone all day. Mary Ann - age 4

17. When you love somebody, your eyelashes go up and down and little stars come out of you. Karen - age 7

18. Love is when mommy sees daddy on the toilet and doesn't think it's gross. Mark - age 6

19. You really shouldn't say I LOVE YOU unless you mean it. But if you mean it, you should say it a lot. People forget. Jessica - age 8

20. And the winner was a 4 year old child whose next door neighbor was an elderly man who had just lost his wife. When the child saw the man cry, the little boy went over into the man's yard and climbed on top of the man's lap and just sat there. When the boy's mother asked him what he'd said to the neighbor, the little boy said, "Nothing, I just helped him cry."

Crabby Old Man
~ Author unknown

What do you see nurses?
What do you see?
What are you thinking when you are looking at me?

A crabby old man…not very wise
uncertain of habit with far away eyes?

Who dribbles his food, and
makes no reply when you say in a loud voice…
"I do wish you'd try!"

Who seems not to notice
the things that you do
and forever is losing
a sock or a shoe.

Who, resisting or not,
let's you do as you will
with bathing and feeding
the lonely day to fill?

Is that what you are thinking,
is that what you see?
Then open your eyes, nurse;
you're not looking at me.

I'll tell you who I am,
as I sit here so still
as I do your bidding,
as I eat your will.

I'm a small child of ten
with a father and a mother,
brothers and sisters who love one another.

A young boy of sixteen
with wings on his feet
dreaming that soon now
  a lover he'll meet.

A groom soon at twenty,
my heart gives a leap
remembering the vows
that I promised to keep.

At twenty-five now I have
young of my own
who need me to guide
and secure a happy home.

A man of thirty,
my young now grown fast,
bound to each other,
with ties that should last.

At forty, my young sons
have grown and are gone,
but my woman's beside me
to see I don't mourn.

At fifty, once more
 the babies play 'round my knee,
 again we know children,
my loved one and me.

Dark days are upon me,
 my wife is now dead.
I look at the future,
I shudder with dread.

For my young are all
rearing young of their own.
and I think of the years
and the love that I've known.

I'm now an old man
and nature is cruel,
"tis jest to make old age
look like a fool.

The body it crumbles,
grace and vigor depart
There is now a stone
where once was a heart.

But inside this old carcass,
a young guy still dwells
and now and again
my battered heart swells.

I remember the joy,
I remember the pain
I think of the years…
all too few, gone too fast,
and accept the stark fact
that nothing can last.

So open your eyes,
people and see
Not a crabby old man.

Look closer, you'll see me!
and I'm loving and living
my life over again.

When an old man died in a geriatric ward of a small hospital near Tampa, Florida, it was thought that he had nothing left of any value. Later when the nurses were going through his meager possessions, they found this poem. Its quality and content so impressed the staff that made copies were made and distributed to every nurse in the hospital. This has since been published in the Christmas edition of the News Magazine of the St. Louis Association of Mental Health. This little old man, with nothing left to give, has authored this poem that now circles the globe.

Scottish Farmer
~ Author unknown

His name was Fleming, and he was a poor Scottish farmer. One day, while trying to make a living for his family, he heard a cry for help coming from a nearby bog. He dropped his tools and ran to the bog.

There, mired to his waist in black muck, was a terrified boy, screaming and struggling to free himself. Farmer Fleming saved the lad from what could have been a slow and terrifying death.

The next day, a fancy carriage pulled up to the Scotsman' sparse surroundings; an elegantly dressed nobleman stepped out of the carriage and introduced himself as the father of the boy Farmer Fleming had saved.

"I want to repay you," said the nobleman. "You saved my son's life."

"No, I can't accept payment for what I did," the Scottish farmer replied, waving off the offer. At that moment, the farmer's own son came to the door of the family hovel.

"Is that your son?" the nobleman asked. "Yes, it is," the farmer replied proudly.

"I'll make you a deal. Let me provide him with the level of education my own son will enjoy. If the lad is anything like his father, he'll no doubt grow up to be a man we both will be proud of." And that he did.

Farmer Fleming's son attended the very best schools and in no time graduated from St. Mary's School in London, and went on to become known throughout the world as the noted Sir Alexander Fleming, the discoverer of Penicillin.

Years afterward, the same nobleman's son who was saved from the bog was stricken with pneumonia. What saved his life this time? Penicillin

The name of the nobleman? Lord Ralph Churchill. His son's name? Sir Winston Churchill.

"Well done is better than well said." ~ Benjamin Franklin

Cherokee Story

There was a young boy in the village that was afraid of everything. The other children in the village teased him and called him "chicken boy." He was most afraid of heights. His grandfather told him that in order to overcome the fear, he had to face it.

One day he decided to climb the cliffs. It was very steep and he was frightened. Every step he took, took him higher and some of the fear dissipated. When he reached the top of the cliff, his fear was gone and he walked to the edge and looked over. From that view he could see his village where everyone was sleeping. He also saw the neighboring warriors coming to attack his village. He screamed as loud as he could, but no one could hear him, he was too far away and they were fast asleep.

He decided to jump off the cliff, trusting that on his way down the village would hear him screaming. When he was close to the bottom, a large white eagle swooped down and lifted him up. Spirit felt that one so brave should be saved. The warrior clan saw the event and knowing the greatness of Spirit in the village came and made peace instead of war.

Offered to me from a friend

"There are two doors in life.
One is marked security and the other freedom.
If you choose the first, you lose both!" ~ Author unknown

Cup of Coffee
~ Author unknown

A group of alumni, all highly established in their respective careers, got together for a visit with their old university professor.

The conversation soon turned to complaints about the endless stress of work and life in general.

Offering his guests coffee, the professor went into the kitchen and soon returned with a large pot of coffee and an eclectic assortment of cups: porcelain, plastic, glass, crystal -- some plain, some expensive, some quite exquisite. Quietly he told them to help themselves to some fresh coffee. When each of his former students had a cup of coffee in hand, the old professor quietly cleared his throat and began to patiently address the small gathering...

You may have noticed that all of the nicer looking cups were taken up first, leaving behind the plainer and cheaper ones; while it is only natural for you to want only the best for yourselves that is actually the source of much of your stress-related problems." He continued..."Be assured that the cup itself adds no quality to the coffee. In fact, the cup merely disguises or dresses up what we drink. What each of you really wanted was coffee, not a cup, but you instinctively went for the best cups... Then you began eyeing each other's cups.'

Now consider this: Life is coffee. Jobs, money, and position in society are merely cups. They are just tools to shape and contain life, and the type of cup we have does not truly define nor change the quality of the life we live. Often, by concentrating only on the cup, we fail to enjoy the coffee that God has provided us... God brews the coffee, but he does not supply the cups. Enjoy your coffee!"

The happiest people don't have the best of everything;
they just make the best of everything...
so please remember: Live simply. Love generously.
Care Deeply. Speak Kindly. Leave the Rest to God.

Breakfast at McDonald's
~Author unknown, but a true story

I am a mother of three (ages 14, 12, 3) and have recently completed my college degree. The last class I had to take was Sociology. The teacher was absolutely inspiring with the qualities that I wish every human being had been graced with. Her last project of the term was called "Smile."

The class was asked to go out and smile at three people and document their reactions. I am a very friendly person and always smile at everyone and say hello anyway, so, I thought this would be a piece of cake, literally.

Soon after we were assigned the project, my husband, youngest son, and I went out to McDonald's one crisp March morning. It was just our way of sharing special playtime with our son. We were standing in line, waiting to be served, when all of a sudden everyone around us began to back away, and then even my husband did.

I did not move an inch... an overwhelming feeling of panic welled up inside of me as I turned to see why they had moved. As I turned around I smelled a horrible "dirty body" smell, and there standing behind me were two poor homeless men. As I looked down at the short gentleman, close to me, he was "smiling". His beautiful sky blue eyes were full of God's Light as he searched for acceptance.

He said, "Good day" as he counted the few coins he had been clutching. The second man fumbled with his hands as he stood behind his friend. I realized the second man was mentally challenged and the blue-eyed gentleman was his salvation. I held my tears as I stood there with them.

The young lady at the counter asked him what they wanted. He said, "Coffee is all Miss" because that was all they could afford. (If they wanted to sit in the restaurant and warm up, they had to buy something. He just wanted to be warm).

Then I really felt it - the compulsion was so great I almost reached out and embraced the little man with the blue eyes.

That is when I noticed all eyes in the restaurant were set on me, judging my every action. I smiled and asked the young lady behind the counter to give me two more breakfast meals on a separate tray. I then walked around the corner to the table that the men had chosen as a resting spot. I put the tray on the table and laid my hand on the blue-eyed gentleman's cold hand. He looked up at me, with tears in his eyes, and said, "Thank you." I leaned over, began to pat his hand and said, "I did not do this for you. God is here working through me to give you hope."

I started to cry as I walked away to join my husband and son. When I sat down my husband smiled at me and said, "That is why God gave you to me, Honey, to give me hope." We held hands for a moment and at that time, we knew that only because of the Grace that we had been given were we able to give. We are not church goers, but we are believers. That day showed me the pure Light of God's sweet love. I returned to college, on the last evening of class, with this story in hand. I turned in "my project" and the instructor read it.

Then she looked up at me and said, "Can I share this?" I slowly nodded as she got the attention of the class.

She began to read and that is when I knew that we as human beings and being part of God share this need to heal people and to be healed. In my own way I had touched the people at McDonald's, my husband, son, instructor, and every soul that shared the classroom on the last night I spent as a college student.

I graduated with one of the biggest lessons I would ever learn: UNCONDITIONAL ACCEPTANCE!

> "**Many people will walk in and out of your life,**
> **but only true friends will leave footprints in your heart.**
> **To handle yourself, use your head.**
> **To handle others, use your heart.**
> **God Gives every bird it's food,**
> **but He does not throw it into its nest.**
> **~author unknown**

Five Lessons About the Way We Treat People

1 - First Important Lesson - Cleaning Lady.

During the second month of college, our professor gave us a pop quiz. I was a conscientious student and had breezed through the questions until I read the last one:

"What is the first name of the woman who cleans the school?" Surely this was some kind of joke. I had seen the cleaning woman several times. She was tall, dark-haired and in her 50's, but how would I know her name?

I handed in my paper, leaving the last question blank. Just before class ended, one student asked if the last question would count toward our quiz grade.

"Absolutely," said the professor... "In your careers, you will meet many people. All are significant. They deserve your attention and care, even if all you do is smile and say "hello."

I've never forgotten that lesson. I also learned her name was Dorothy.

2. Second Important Lesson - Pickup in the Rain

One night, at 11:30 p.m., an older African American woman was standing on the side of an Alabama highway trying to endure a lashing rain storm. Her car had broken down and she desperately needed a ride.

Soaking wet, she decided to flag down the next car. A young white man stopped to help her, generally unheard of in those conflict-filled 1960's. The man took her to safety, helped her get assistance and put her into a taxicab.

She seemed to be in a big hurry, but wrote down his address and thanked him.

Seven days went by and a knock came on the man's door. To his surprise, a giant console color TV was delivered to his home.

A special note was attached. It read:

"Thank you so much for assisting me on the highway the other night. The rain drenched not only my clothes, but also my spirits.

Then you came along. Because of you, I was able to make it to my dying husband's bedside just before he passed away...

God bless you for helping me and unselfishly serving others."

Sincerely,
Mrs. Nat King Cole

3. Third Important Lesson - Always remember those Who serve.
In the days when an ice cream sundae cost much less, a 10-year-old boy entered a hotel coffee shop and sat at a table. A waitress put a glass of water in front of him.

"How much is an ice cream sundae?" he asked.

"Fifty cents," replied the waitress.

The little boy pulled his hand out of his pocket and studied the coins in it.

"Well, how much is a plain dish of ice cream?" he inquired.

By now more people were waiting for a table and the waitress was growing impatient.

"Thirty-five cents," she brusquely replied.

The little boy again counted his coins. "I'll have the plain ice cream," he said.

The waitress brought the ice cream, put the bill on the table and walked away. The boy finished the ice cream, paid the cashier and left.

When the waitress came back, she began to cry as she wiped down the table; there, placed neatly beside the empty dish, were two nickels and five pennies.

You see, he couldn't have the sundae, because he had to have enough left to leave her a tip.

4. Fourth Important Lesson. - The obstacle in Our Path.

In ancient times, a King had a boulder placed on a roadway. Then he hid himself and watched to see if anyone would remove the huge rock. Some of the King's' wealthiest merchants and courtiers came by and simply walked around it. Many loudly blamed the King for not keeping the roads clear, but none did anything about getting the stone out of the way.

Then a peasant came along carrying a load of vegetables. Upon approaching the boulder, the peasant laid down his burden and tried to move the stone to the side of the road. After much pushing and straining, he finally succeeded.

After the peasant picked up his load of vegetables, he noticed a purse lying in the road where the boulder had been. The purse contained many gold coins and a note from the King indicating that the gold was for the person who removed the boulder from the roadway.

The peasant learned what many of us never understand!

Every obstacle presents an opportunity to improve our condition.

5. Fifth Important Lesson - Giving When it Counts...

Many years ago, when I worked as a volunteer at a hospital, I got to know a little girl named Liz who was suffering from a rare & serious disease. Her only chance of recovery appeared to be a blood transfusion from her 5-year old brother, who had miraculously survived the same disease and had developed the antibodies needed to combat the illness.

The doctor explained the situation to her little brother, and asked the little boy if he would be willing to give his blood to his sister. I saw him hesitate for only a moment before taking a deep breath and saying, "Yes I'll do it if it will save her."

As the transfusion progressed, he lay in bed next to his sister and smiled, as we all did, seeing the color returning to her cheek. Then his face grew pale and his smile faded. He looked up at the doctor and asked with a trembling voice, "Will I start to die right away?"

Being young, the little boy had misunderstood the doctor; he thought he was going to have to give his sister all of his blood in order to save her.

Believing You Can
by Will Craig

A young man fell asleep during math class. He woke up as the bell rang, looked at the blackboard, and copied down the two problems that were there. He assumed they were the homework for the night. He went home and labored the rest of the afternoon and into the evening knowing if he didn't complete the work he would surely fail the class.

He couldn't figure out either one but he kept trying for the rest of the week. Finally, he got the answer to one and brought it to class. The teacher was absolutely stunned. The boy feared he had done too little, too late. It turned out the problem he solved was supposedly unsolvable.

Power Commanders
How did he do it? He was able to do what was thought to be impossible because he believed it was possible. He not only believed it was possible, he believed that if he didn't solve it he would fail the class. Had he known the problem was unsolvable he could never have done it.

Beliefs are the commanders of our brain. When we believe something is true, we literally go into the state of its being true. Handled effectively, beliefs can be the most powerful forces for creating good in our lives.

The Birth of Excellence
Beliefs control our destiny: The belief we have in ourselves... the belief we have in our clients... the belief others have in us. The birth of excellence begins with the awareness that our beliefs are a choice.

Beliefs are the compass and map that guide us to our goals. Believe you can do something -OR- believe you can't and you'll be right every time.

Enough
~Author unknown

I wish you enough sun to keep your attitude bright no matter how gray the day may appear.

I wish you enough rain to
appreciate the sun even more.
I wish you enough happiness
to keep your spirit alive and everlasting.

I wish you enough pain so that even the smallest of joys in life may appear bigger.

I wish you enough gain to satisfy your wanting.

I wish you enough loss to appreciate all that you possess.

I wish you enough hellos to get you through the final good-bye.

They say it takes a minute to find a special person, an hour to appreciate them, a day to love them, but an entire life to forget them.

Jasmine: A true story

In 2003, police in Warwickshire, England, opened a garden shed and found a whimpering, cowering dog. The dog had been locked in the shed and abandoned. It was dirty and malnourished, and had quite clearly been abused.

In an act of kindness, the police took the dog, which was a female greyhound, to the Nuneaton Warwickshire Wildlife Sanctuary, which is run by a man named Geoff Grewcock, and known as a haven for animals abandoned, orphaned, or otherwise in need.

Geoff and the other sanctuary staff went to work with two aims: to restore the dog to full health, and to win her trust. It took several weeks, but eventually both goals were achieved. They named her Jasmine, and they started to think about finding her an adoptive home.

Jasmine, however, had other ideas. No one quite remembers how it came about, but Jasmine started welcoming all animal arrivals at the sanctuary. It would not matter if it were a puppy, a fox cub, a rabbit or, any other lost or hurting animal. Jasmine would just peer into the box or cage and, when and where possible, deliver a welcoming lick.

Geoff relates one of the early incidents. "We had two puppies that had been abandoned by a nearby railway line; one was a Lakeland Terrier cross and another was a Jack Russell Doberman cross. They were tiny when they arrived at the centre, and Jasmine approached them and grabbed one by the scruff of the neck in her mouth and put him on the settee. Then she fetched the other one and sat down with them, cuddling them."

"But she is like that with all of our animals, even the rabbits. She takes all the stress out of them, and it helps them to not only feel close to her, but to settle into their new surroundings. She has done the same with the fox and badger cubs, she licks the rabbits and guinea pigs, and even lets the birds perch on the bridge of her nose."

Jasmine, the timid, abused, deserted waif, became the animal sanctuary's resident surrogate mother, a role for which she might have been born. The list of orphaned and abandoned youngsters she has cared for comprises five fox cubs, four badger cubs, fifteen chicks, eight guinea pigs, two stray puppies and fifteen rabbits - and one roe deer fawn. Tiny Bramble, eleven weeks old, was found semi-conscious in a field. Upon arrival at the sanctuary, Jasmine cuddled up to her to keep her warm, and then went into the full foster-mum role. Jasmine the greyhound showers Bramble the roe deer with affection, and makes sure nothing is matted."

(A reported story on the internet, source unknown)

"**Money can buy you a good dog
but it won't buy the wag of his tail.**
Author unknown

**A dog is the only thing on earth that loves
you more than he loves himself."**
Josh Billings

THE FORK!
~Author unknown

There was a woman who had been diagnosed with a terminal illness and had been given three months to live. So as she was getting her things "in order," she contacted her pastor and had him come to her house to discuss certain aspects of her final wishes. She told him which songs she wanted sung at the service and what scriptures she would like read, and what outfit she wanted to be buried in. The woman also requested to be buried with her favorite Bible. Everything was in order and the pastor was preparing to leave when the woman suddenly remembered something very important to her. "There's one more thing, she said excitedly. "What's that?" Came the pastor's reply. "This is very important," the woman continued. "I want to be buried with a fork in my right hand."

The pastor stood looking at the woman, not knowing quite what to say. "That surprises you, doesn't it?" the woman asked. "Well, to be honest, I'm puzzled by the request," said the pastor. The woman explained. "In all my years of attending church socials and potluck dinners, I always remember that when the dishes of the main course were being cleared, someone would inevitably lean over and say, 'Keep your fork.' It was my favorite part because I knew that something better was coming...like velvety chocolate cake or deep dish apple pie. Something wonderful, and with substance! So, I just want people to see me there in that casket with a fork in my hand and I want them to wonder "What's with the fork?'. Then I want you to tell them: "Keep your fork....the best is yet to come".

The pastor's eyes welled up with tears of joy as he hugged the woman good-bye. He knew this would be one of the last times he would see her before her death. But he also knew that the woman had a better grasp of heaven than he did. She KNEW that something better was coming.

At the funeral people were walking by the woman's casket and they saw the pretty dress she was wearing another favorite Bible and the fork placed in her right hand. Over and over, the pastor heard the question "What's with the fork?" And over and over he smiled. During his message, the pastor told the people of the conversation he had with the woman shortly before she died. He also told them about the fork and about what it symbolized to her.

The pastor told the people how he could not stop thinking about the fork and told them that they probably would not be able to stop thinking about it either. He was right. So the next time you reach down for your fork, let it remind you, oh so gently, that the best is yet to come.

This is a quiz for people who know everything!
~Author unknown

These are not trick questions. They are straight questions with straight answers

1. Name the one sport in which neither the spectators nor the participants know the score or the leader until the contest ends.

2. What famous North American landmark is constantly moving backward?

3. Of all vegetables, only two can live to produce on their own for several growing seasons. All other vegetables must be replanted every year. What are the only two perennial vegetables?

4. What fruit has its seeds on the outside?

5. In many liquor stores, you can buy pear brandy, with a real pear inside the bottle. The pear is whole and ripe, and the bottle is genuine; it hasn't been cut in any way. How did the pear get inside the bottle?

6. Only three words in standard English begin with the letters ' dw' and they are all common words.

Name two of them.
7. There are 14 punctuation marks in English grammar. Can you name at least half of them?

8. Name the only vegetable or fruit that is never sold frozen, canned, processed, cooked, or in any other form except fresh.

9. Name 6 or more things that you can wear on your feet beginning with the letter 'S.'

Answers to Quiz:

1. The one sport in which neither the spectators nor the participants know the score or the leader until the contest ends: Boxing

2. North American landmark constantly moving backward. Niagara Falls (The rim is worn down about two and a half feet each year because of the millions of gallons of water that rush over it every minute.)

3. Only two vegetables that can live to produce on their own for several growing seasons; asparagus and rhubarb

4. The fruit with its seeds on the outside ...Strawberry.

5. How did the pear get inside the brandy bottle? It grew inside the bottle.

   (The bottles are placed over pear buds when they are small, and are wired in place on the tree.
   The bottle is left in place for the entire growing season. When the pears are ripe, they are snipped off at the stems.)

6. Three English words beginning with dw Dwarf, dwell and dwindle.

7. Fourteen punctuation marks in English grammar: Period, comma, colon, semicolon, dash, hyphen, apostrophe, question mark, exclamation point, quotation marks, brackets, parenthesis, braces, and ellipses.

8. The only vegetable or fruit never sold frozen, canned, processed, cooked, or in any other form but fresh. Lettuce.

9. Six or more things you can wear on your feet beginning with 'S': Shoes, socks, sandals, sneakers, slippers, skis, skates, snowshoes, stockings, stilts.

We must have a little humor as we go through our day, so this is included with that intent, enjoy!

Dear Dogs and Cats
~ Author unknown

The dishes with the paw prints are yours and contain your food. The other dishes are mine and contain my food. Please note, placing a paw print in the middle of my plate of food does not stake a claim for it becoming your food and dish, nor do I find that aesthetically pleasing in slightest.

The stairway was not designed by NASCAR and is not a racetrack. Beating me to the bottom is not the object. Tripping me doesn't help because I fall faster than you can run.

I cannot buy anything bigger than a king sized bed. I am very sorry about this. Do not think I will continue sleeping on the couch to ensure your comfort. Dogs and cats can actually curl up in a ball when they sleep. It is not necessary to sleep perpendicular to each other stretched out to the fullest extent possible. I also know that sticking tails straight out and having tongues hanging out the other end to maximize space is nothing but sarcasm.

For the last time, there is no secret exit from the bathroom. If by some miracle I beat you there and manage to get the door shut, it is not necessary to claw, whine, meow, and try to turn the knob or get your paw under the edge and try to pull the door open. I must exit through the same door I entered. Also, I have been using the bathroom for years -- canine or feline attendance is not required.

The proper order is kiss me, then go smell the other dog or cat's butt.
I cannot stress this enough!

To All Non-Pet Owners Who Visit and
Like to Complain About Our Pets
~Author unknown, but appreciated

1. They live here. You don't.
2. If you don't want their hair on your clothes, stay off the furniture. That's why they call it 'fur'niture.
3. I like my pets a lot better than I like most people.
4. To you, they are an animal. To me, he/she is an adopted son/daughter who is short, hairy, walks on all fours and doesn't speak clearly.

Remember: Dogs and cats are better than kids because they:

1. Eat less

2. Don't ask for money all the time

3. Are easier to train

4. Normally come when called

5. Never ask to drive the car

6. Don't hang out with drug-using friends

7. Don't smoke or drink

8. Don't have to buy the latest fashions

9. Don't want to wear your clothes

10. Don't need a gazillion dollars for college, and

11. If they get pregnant, you can sell their children!!

"Compassion is that which makes the heart of the good move at the pain of others. Thus, it is called compassion. It is called compassion because it shelters & embraces the distressed." - Dalai Lama

Why Women Should Vote
~Author unknown

This is the story of our Grandmothers and Great-grandmothers, as they lived only 90 years ago. Remember, it was not until 1920 that women were granted the right to go to the polls and vote. The women were innocent and defenseless, but they were jailed nonetheless for picketing the White House, carrying signs asking for the vote.

"...And by the end of the night, they were barely alive. Forty prison guards wielding clubs and their warden's blessing went on a rampage against the 33 women wrongly convicted of 'obstructing sidewalk traffic.' They beat Lucy Burn, chained her hands to the cell bars above her head and left her hanging for the night, bleeding and gasping for air. They hurled Dora Lewis into a dark cell, smashed her head against an iron bed and knocked her out cold. Her cellmate, Alice Cosu, thought Lewis was dead and suffered a heart attack. Additional affidavits describe the guards grabbing, dragging, beating, choking, slamming, pinching, twisting and kicking the women.

Thus unfolded the 'Night of Terror' on Nov. 15, 1917, when the warden at the Occoquan Workhouse in Virginia ordered his guards to teach a lesson to the suffragists imprisoned there because they dared to picket the White House for the right to vote.

For weeks, the women's only water came from an open pail. Their food--all of it colorless slop--was infested with worms. When one of the leaders, Alice Paul, embarked on a hunger strike, they tied her to a chair, forced a tube down her throat and poured liquid into her until she vomited. She was tortured like this for weeks until word was smuggled out to the press."

My note:
As of 2013 the Equal Rights Amendment calling for women to have the same equal rights as men has never been ratified by the 38 states required by Congress to do so.

"Changes"
~Dr. Maya Angelou

When I was in my younger days,

I weighed a few pounds less,

I needn't hold my tummy *in* to wear a belted dress.

But now that I am older, I've set my body free;

There's the comfort of elastic,

Where once my waist would be.

Inventor of those high-heeled shoes

My feet have not forgiven;

I have to wear a nine now,

But used to wear a seven.

And how about those pantyhose-

They're sized by weight, you see,

How come when I put them on

The crotch is at my knee?

I need to wear these glasses

As the print's been getting smaller;

And it wasn't very long ago I know that I was taller.

Though my hair has turned to gray and my skin no longer fits,

On the inside, I'm the same old me,

It's the outside's changed a bit.

A Dad's Poem
~Author unknown

Her hair was up in a pony tail, her favorite dress tied with a bow.

Today was Daddy's Day at school, and she couldn't wait to go.

But her mommy tried to tell her, that she probably should stay home.

Why the kids might not understand, if she went to school alone.

But she was not afraid; she knew just what to say; what to tell her classmates of why he wasn't there today.

But still her mother worried, for her to face this day alone.

And that was why once again, she tried to keep her daughter home.

But the little girl went to school, eager to tell them all. About a dad she'd never see a dad who never calls.

There were daddies along the wall in back, for everyone to meet.

Children squirming impatiently, anxious in their seats.

One by one the teacher called a student from the class to introduce their daddy, as seconds slowly passed.

At last the teacher called her name, every child turned to stare. Each of them was searching, for a man who wasn't there.

"Where's her daddy at?" she heard a boy call out. "She probably doesn't have one, "another student dared to shout.

And from somewhere near the back, she heard a daddy say, "Looks like another deadbeat dad, too busy to waste his day."

The words did not offend her, as she smiled up at her Mom, and looked back at her teacher, who told her to go on.

And with hands behind her back, slowly she began to speak, and out from the mouth of a child, came words incredibly unique. "My Daddy couldn't be here, because he lives so far away.

But I know he wishes he could be, since this is such a special day. and though you cannot meet him, I wanted you to know all about my daddy, and how much he loves me so.

He loved to tell me stories he taught me to ride my bike. He surprised me with pink roses, and taught me to fly a kite.

We used to share fudge sundaes, and ice cream in a cone.

And though you cannot see him, I'm not standing here alone. "Cause my daddy's always with me, even though we are apart I know because he told me, he'll forever be in my heart"

With that, her little hand reached up, and lay across her chest. feeling her own heartbeat, beneath her favorite dress.

And from somewhere in the crowd of dads, her mother stood in tears proudly watching her daughter, who was wise beyond her years.

For she stood up for the love of a man not in her life. Doing what was best for her, doing what was right.

And when she dropped her hand back down, staring straight into the crowd she finished with a voice so soft, but its message clear and loud.

"I love my daddy very much, he's my shining star.

And if he could, he'd be here, but heaven's just too far.

You see he was a fireman and died just this past year

When airplanes hit the towers and taught Americans to fear. But sometimes when I close my eyes, it's like he never went away."

And then she closed her eyes, and saw him there that day.

And to her mother's amazement, she witnessed with surprise.

A room full of daddies and children, all starting to close their eyes.

Who knows what they saw before them, who knows what they felt inside; perhaps for merely a second, they saw him at her side.

I know you're with me Daddy," to the silence she called out.

And what happened next made believers, of those once filled with doubt.

Not one in that room could explain it, for each of their eyes had been closed.

But there on the desk beside her, was a fragrant long-stemmed pink rose.

And a child was blessed, if only for a moment, by the love of her shining bright star.

And given the gift of believing that heaven is never too far.

"You gain strength, courage and confidence by every experience in which you really stop to look fear in the face. You are able to say to yourself, 'I lived through this horror. I can take the next thing that comes along. 'You must do the thing you think you cannot do."
~ Eleanor Roosevelt, "This 'n That"

Declaration of Independence
~Author unknown

Have you ever wondered what happened to the 56 men who signed the Declaration of Independence?

Five signers were captured by the British as traitors, and tortured before they died.

Twelve had their homes ransacked and burned.

Two lost their sons serving in the Revolutionary Army; another had two sons captured.

Nine of the 56 fought and died from wounds or hardships of the Revolutionary War.

They signed and they pledged their lives, their fortunes, and their sacred honor.

What kind of men were they?

Twenty-four were lawyers and jurists.

Eleven were merchants.

Nine were farmers and large plantation owners; men of means, well educated.

But they signed the Declaration of Independence knowing full well that the penalty would be death if they were captured.

Carter Braxton of Virginia, a wealthy planter and trader, saw his ships swept from the seas by the British Navy. He sold his home and properties to pay his debts, and died in rags.

Thomas McKeam was so hounded by the British that he was forced to move his family almost constantly. He served in the Congress without pay, and his family was kept in hiding. His possessions were taken from him, and poverty was his reward.

Vandals or soldiers looted the properties of Dillery, Hall, Clymer, Walton, Gwinnett, Heyward, Ruttledge, and Middleton.

At the battle of Yorktown, Thomas Nelson Jr, noted that the British General Cornwallis had taken over the Nelson home for his headquarters. He quietly urged General George Washington to open fire. The home was destroyed, and Nelson died bankrupt.

Francis Lewis had his home and properties destroyed. The enemy jailed his wife, and she died within a few months.

John Hart was driven from his wife's bedside as she was dying. Their 13 children fled for their lives. His fields and his gristmill were laid to waste. For more than a year he lived in forests and caves, returning home to find his wife dead and his children vanished. A few weeks later he died from exhaustion and a broken heart.

Norris and Livingston suffered similar fates.

One Stormy Night
~Author unknown

One stormy night many years ago, an elderly man and his wife entered the lobby of a small hotel in Philadelphia. Trying to get out of the rain, the couple approached the front desk hoping to get some shelter for the night. "Could you possibly give us a room here?" the husband asked.

The clerk, a friendly man with a winning smile, looked at the couple and explained that there were three conventions in town. "All of our rooms are taken," the clerk said. "But I can't send a nice couple like you out into the rain at one o'clock in the morning. Would you perhaps be willing to sleep in my room? It's not exactly a suite, but it will be good enough to make you folks comfortable for the night."

When the couple declined, the young man pressed on. "Don't worry about me. I'll make out just fine," the clerk told them.

So the couple agreed. As he paid his bill the next morning, the elderly man said to the clerk, "You are the kind of manager who should be the boss of the best hotel in the United States. Maybe someday I'll build one for you."

The clerk looked at them and smiled. The three of them had a good laugh. As they drove away, the elderly couple agreed that the helpful clerk was indeed exceptional, as finding people who are both friendly and helpful isn't easy.

Two years passed. The clerk had almost forgotten the incident when he received a letter from the old man; it recalled that stormy night and enclosed a round-trip ticket to New York, asking the young man to pay them a visit. The old man met him in New York, and led him to the corner of Fifth Avenue and 34th Street. He then pointed to a great new building there, a palace of reddish stone, with turrets and watchtowers thrusting up to the sky. "That," said the older man, "is the hotel I have just built for you to manage."

"You must be joking," the young man said.

"I can assure you I am not," said the older man, a sly smile playing around his mouth. The older man's name was William Waldorf Astor, and the magnificent structure was the original Waldorf-Astoria Hotel.

The young clerk who became its first manager was George C. Boldt. This young clerk never foresaw the turn of events that would lead him to become the manager of one of the world's most glamorous hotels.

"Treat everyone with love, grace and respect, and you cannot fail!"

Heart Prints
~Author unknown

Whatever our hands touch-
We leave fingerprints!
On walls, on furniture
On doorknobs, dishes, books.
There's no escape.
As we touch we leave our identity.

Oh God, wherever I go today
Help me leave heart prints!
Heart prints of compassion
Of understanding and love.

Heart prints of kindness
And genuine concern.
May my heart touch a lonely neighbor
Or a runaway daughter
Or an anxious mother
Or perhaps an aged grandfather.

Lord, send me out today
To leave heart prints.
And if someone should say,
"I felt your touch,"
May that one sense YOUR LOVE
Touching through ME.

Famous Quotes on Assorted Subjects

"Happiness lies in the joy of achievement and the thrill of creative effort." --Franklin D. Roosevelt

~

"Each of us must do massive right thinking, take massive right action and get massive right results, right here, right now."
~ Mark Victor Hansen

~

"The secret of success in life is for a man to be ready for his opportunity when it comes." ~ Benjamin Disraeli

~

"When you have decided what you believe, what you feel must be done, have the courage to stand alone and be counted." ~ Eleanor Roosevelt

~

"The world doesn't come to the clever folks, it comes to the stubborn, obstinate, one-idea-at-a-time people." ~ Mary Roberts Rinehart

~

"When you align your values with action expect a masterpiece."
~unknown

~

"It concerns us to know the purpose we seek in life, for then, like archers at a definite mark, we shall be more likely to attain what we want." ~ Aristotle

~

"Reach for the sky, because if you should happen to miss, you'll still be among the stars." ~ Touched By An Angel TV program

~

"The leader who would create a vision sufficiently compelling to motivate associates to superior performances must draw on the intuitive mind." ~J. Naisbitt & P. Aburdene

~

Seven blunders of the world that leads to violence: wealth without work, pleasure without conscience, knowledge without character, commerce without morality, science without humanity, worship without sacrifice, politics without principle. ~Mahatma Gandhi

~

"You need not meditate like I do, but meditate so that the love in your heart dwells in the house of your Creator." ~Dr. Jane Cundy

~

"Pack for where you are going, not where you have been!"
~Dr. Jane Cundy

~

"You can only wake up from a dream once!" ~Unknown

~

"Champions are people with a poorly developed sense of fear and no concept of the odds against them. They are a bit unrealistic in how they see life as they don't reason with reality. They make the impossible happen and never considered it impossible." ~Grant Cardone

~

"If your actions inspire others to dream more, learn more, do more and become more, you are a leader."~John Quincy Adams

~

"Take away my people, but leave my factories, and soon grass will grow on the factory floors. Take away my factories, but leave my people and soon we will have a new and better factory."
~ Andrew Carnegie

~

"Experience the business behind the magic." ~Walt Disney

~

"Courage is the main quality of leadership in my opinion… usually it implies some risk."~ Walt Disney"

~

"Any society that would give up a little liberty to gain a little security will deserve neither and lose both." ~ Benjamin Franklin

~

"Words may show a man's wit, but actions his meaning."
~ Benjamin Franklin

~

"It is not our differences that divide us. It is our inability to recognize, accept, and celebrate those differences."~ Audre Lorde

~

"I'm fulfilled in what I do...I never thought that a lot of money or fine clothes--the finer things in life--would make you happy. My happiness is to be filled in a spiritual sense." ~ Coretta Scott King

~

"People who cannot invent and reinvent themselves must be content with borrowed postures, secondhand ideas, fitting in instead of standing out." ~Warren G. Bennis

~

"Happiness is not something ready made... It comes from your own actions." ~Dalai Lama

"There are two doors in life. One is marked security and the other freedom. If you choose the first, you lose both!" ~unknown

~

"If you realize that you have enough, you are truly rich."
~Tao Te Ching

~

"So let us not be blind to our differences--but let us also direct attention to our common interests and to the means by which those differences can be resolved." ~ John F. Kennedy

~

"The structure of world peace cannot be the work of one man, or one party, or one nation. It must be a peace which rests on the cooperative effort of the whole world" ~ Franklin D. Roosevelt

~

"The best and most beautiful things in the world cannot be seen or even touched. They must be felt with the heart." ~ Helen Keller

~

"A people that values its privileges above its principles soon loses both." ~Dwight Eisenhower

~

"Love has nothing to do with what you are expecting to get, it's what you are expected to give — which is everything."~ Unknown

~

"You can't shake hands with a clenched fist"~Indira Gandhi.

~

"What you leave behind is not what is engraved in stone monuments, but what is woven into the lives of others."~ Pericles

~

"Intolerance has been the curse of every age and state" ~ Unknown

~

"Too often we underestimate the power of a touch, a smile, a kind word, a listening ear, an honest compliment, or the smallest act of caring, all of which have the potential to turn a life around." ~Unknown

~

"Be kinder than necessary, for everyone you meet is fighting some kind of battle"~ Unknown

~

"Great spirits have always encountered violent opposition from mediocre minds. ~ Albert Einstein

~

"Only those who dare to fail greatly can ever achieve greatly."
~ Robert F. Kennedy

~

"The greatest weapon against stress is our ability to choose one thought over another." ~ William James

~

"There are only two ways to live your life. One is as though nothing is a miracle. The other is as though everything is a miracle." ~ Albert Einstein

~

"Conflict is the largest reducible cost in organizations today, and the least recognized." ~Dan Dana

~

"Faith is taking the first step even when you don't see the whole staircase." ~ Martin Luther King, Jr.

~

"Anyone can become angry. That is easy. But to be angry with the right person, to the right degree, at the right time, for the right purpose, and in the right way--that is not easy." ~ Aristotle

~

"They always say that time changes things, but you actually have to change them yourself."~ Andy Warhol

~

"The mind has exactly the same power as the hands: not merely to grasp the world, but to change it." ~Colin Wilson

~

"What this power is, I cannot say. All I know is that it exists . . . and it becomes available only when you are in that state of mind in which you know EXACTLY what you want . . . and are fully determined not to quit until you get it." ~ Alexander Graham Bell

~

"Before you embark on a journey of revenge, dig two graves" ~Confucius

~

"Personal empowerment means, at its core, going for what you want without reserve or apology." ~ Unknown

~

"Things behave in alignment with how the observer expects them to behave, so as we change our collective story about the state of the world, the state of the world also changes."~ Arjuna Ardagh

~

"The most important trip you may take in life is meeting people halfway"~ Henry Boye."
"Attitude is everything. As the saying goes; "The kind of life you will have isn't determined by what happens to you, it's determined by your reaction to what happens to you." ~ Unknown

~

"There are two possible outcomes: If the result confirms the hypothesis, then you've made a measurement. If the result is contrary to the hypothesis, then you've made a discovery."
~ *Margaret Young*

~

"A human being is a part of a whole, called by us the "universe," a part limited in time and space. He experiences himself, his thoughts and feelings as separate from himself – a kind of optical delusion of his consciousness. This delusion is a kind of prison for us, restricting us to our personal desires and to affection for a few persons nearest to us. Our task must be to free ourselves from this prison by widening our circles of compassion to embrace all living creatures and the whole of nature in its beauty." ~ *Albert Einstein*

~

"One should use as little energy as possible staying in mediocrity."
~ Peter Drucker

~

"The moment your fear of not trying overrides your fear of failure in that one spectacular moment -- the pathway to success is cleared of all debris and you take the first steps toward a magnificent future. Never let fear stop you when it can just as easily push you forward." ~ Unknown

~

An Exercise of Faith
"Even if you feel like you don't know what you're doing, follow through with your plan. It's an exercise of faith. Connect the dots, close in on goals, and seize the chance to test your theory. With a few more steps forward, suddenly the image of your future clicks into focus."
~Author Unknown

~

"We tend to live up to our own expectations."~ Earl Nightingale

~

"In periods where there is no leadership, society stands still. Progress occurs when courageous, skillful leaders seize the opportunity to change things for the better." ~ Harry S. Truman

~

"When the desire is strong enough, the facts don't matter." ~unknown

~

"Humor opens the door that allows your heart to shine"
~Dr. Jane Cundy

~

"Prosperity is a state of heart." ~Dr. Jane Cundy

"God does not command that we do great things...Only little things with Great Love." "Mother Teresa"

~

Today
Adapted by Dr. Jane F Cundy

.... I wish you a day of ordinary miracles

.... A fresh pot of coffee you didn't make yourself

.... An unexpected phone call from an old friend

.... Green stoplights on your way to work

.... The fastest line at the grocery store

.... A good sing-along song on the radio

.... Your keys right where you left them

.... One of God's angles to surprise you

.... The smile of a child

.... And the Love of a dog

Selections of Inspirations and Tips

from

"Your Coffee Break for the Brain"

Newsletters

2008-2012

Creativity

Whenever we get locked into fears, doubts or indecision we have shut down the greatest tool we have, our creativity.

It is our creative genius, our uniqueness that sets us apart from the animal kingdom and allows for progress in business, science, math, and music. How creative are you and what is your next "AH HA" waiting to happen.

Share your genius with those whom you trust to support you and cheer you on. You never know where your next miracle is hiding!

~

Your Inspirational Cause

Getting more from others is certainly a good way of increasing productivity. But how do you go about turning on the hearts as well as the minds of others? Sun Tzu's art of war suggests that we first must look at our motivations for setting our objectives. Objectives that are rooted in greed, selfishness, ego maintenance or desperation are unlikely to motivate others to take action whilst objectives that are done in the right way for the right reason will flick that mysterious switch and turn people on. Look for objectives that will benefit something bigger than yourself and you will be on the right path. Chin-ning Chu advocates a winning strategy is one that is essentially good, creative, innovative, joyful, brilliant, sweet or ecstatic!

~

Attitude Equals Altitude

My friends laugh at me when I tell them that their attitude in life is measured by their altitude.

In these difficult days of economic turmoil, downsizing of everything from paychecks and housing to the amount of groceries we can bring home, people's attitudes are diminishing along with the dollar.

When our attitudes diminish the results are realized in our jobs and our relationships, and it doesn't take long. How has your attitude changed lately?

This is the perfect time to raise your altitude, think higher thoughts, write in your gratitude journal, find joy in the little things and I promise your personal relationships will prosper and your financial economy will grow along with it.

The higher your altitude, the more positive your attitude becomes, it can't not work! Spread Joy!

A Little Exercise We Can All Use

Remember to breathe when things get rough. Then STOP! Take a deep breath; allow it to flow through your body with love and lightness. Exhale releasing all of your stress along with it. Repeat this as often as necessary. It works.

~

Speaking Truth; Even When it is Uncomfortable!

When my children were small, they would, at times, embellish the truth into such remarkable stories that anything resembling what actually took place was merely coincidence.

I have noticed in the business world, and throughout my years of coaching and consulting, that there are cases where these habits never left one's childhood. It tends to especially show up in marketing and sales.

"Watch Your Thoughts, They Become Words, Watch Your Words, They Become Actions. Watch Your Actions; They Become Habits. Watch Your Habits; They Become Character. Watch Your Character; It Becomes Your Destiny!

This quote hangs on the wall in my office because I believe it to be so valuable that I never choose to forget to assist my clients with the core truth of their situation; even when it would sometimes be easier to color it somewhat.

This trait of unbridled truth is what brings each of us more clients, increases our sales and helps us to retain clients. In these difficult economic times, it might be easier to revert to childish ways, yet it can be much more costly in the long run.

~

The "Cadet Prayer"
Repeated during chapel services at the U.S. Military Academy

"Make us to choose the harder right instead of the easier wrong, and never to be content with a half truth when the whole truth can be won. Endow us with the courage that is born of loyalty to all that is noble and worthy, that scorns to compromise with vice and injustice and knows no fear when truth and right are in jeopardy."

Dreams

Perhaps this is the season when we hear more about dreams than usual. Our children or grandchildren are dreaming about all of the gifts they may receive from Santa or whomever they believe in at this time. We are perhaps dreaming about a new relationship, or how the one we are in will be perfect for the holidays; others simply dream that they have someone with them during these busy and sometimes chaotic final days of the year.

In business, many of us are praying that our fiscal year will end greater than last and perhaps this year specifically, some may be dreaming that there is still a job or that the balance sheet will actually show a profit.

Whatever the case for you, you can weather these turbulent times with clear and focused dreams of what you are choosing for the New Year. It is time to focus on the positive, be grateful for whatever blessings have come your way, and set some clear and precise dreams and goals for the future. Whatever you are choosing for your next steps, make them as fun filled, positive and loving as you can possibly imagine.

Remember; 98% of your fears never come true anyway, so why not focus on the best of life for you, your family and your future?

Some Tips for Success

- Be determined.
- Finish what you start.
- Know your dream.
- Stay positive.
- Look at problems as opportunities.
- Treat your co-workers and colleagues as first time meetings.
- Listen only to those whom you trust and respect.
- Be inspired by greatness...yours and others.
- Dream bigger and in vibrant color, make it real.
- Be grateful for those who love you.
- Have a coach in your corner~ two heads are always better than one. It is good for your sanity!
- Keep your sense of humor~ it lowers your blood pressure.
- Remember the 80/20 rule; not everyone is a sprinter or out for the world's record!
- Do your best to stay focused. One step at a time still gets you there.
- Remember to look up and give thanks for what you have.

Blueprints for Action

I have not always been the best at pre-planning what I was going to do next. Sometimes just the thought of having a map for directions or creating a plan for what was to take place next was too limiting for me, and frankly a bit boring.

For instance, if I am going to take a road trip and I have gone in that general direction before, I most likely will just get in the car and go. The discovery and spontaneity is part of the journey and the excitement.

Last month I drove from New Mexico to Massachusetts with my son as he was moving and I didn't want him to make that long drive all alone; besides I have made it many times and "knew" where I was going.

In business, however I usually do just the opposite. When I am going to speak to a group, or present a workshop the planning norm is a 3:1 ratio. Many times I spend three hours of prep for each hour of presenting.

If I have a new coaching or consulting client, the time spent in preparation can be similar, though not always. Generally once I know the client, I have a pretty good idea which set of tools to use and how often to spend more time planning for the unknown.

How do <u>you</u> prepare for success and still maintain the excitement?

~

Listening

I can't begin to tell you how many people suffer from the affliction of not listening. The number one issue in today's society is <u>the desire to be heard</u>, yet most of us are busy thinking about what "we" want to say; or how whatever "you" are telling me is not as important as what "I" have to say.

Many times when you share an experience the listener is thinking about the story that they have to tell that is "one up" from your experience. It is much like the person who wants to show you their scar from surgery, and you say that's nothing! Wait until I show you my scar! *(It is like my job is bigger than your job.) I'm inviting you to offer the same respect to others that you request.*

Chickens, Hawks and Eagles

I have been watching a lot of people lately and noticing the difference in how they approach their work.

There are some individuals who I interact with occasionally that have all of the "right ingredients;" meaning that they are very professional, have great personalities and also have a quasi desire to really make a difference in their line of work. However, it seems that they never get off of "GO." They sort of get started and then run out of gas or desire or simply know-how to get the job done.

The next type of people that I run into have what it takes as well; they are excited about the future, they put their all into getting to the next phase of their climb to success, they see the results of their journey just ahead of them and then something happens. They either decide that they won't make it, or it is too difficult to go the last few miles or they simply run out of gas. Whatever the reason they stop short of what they said that their dream was.

For some there is an unbridled enthusiasm that takes over. It never seems to be work, just fun. They get up every day with new ideas and new ways of going over the top. These people don't really think of the end results; they are so much in the joy of the journey that the journey becomes the fuel to keep going.

That is the dream. It is the ability to make a difference in each person's life that is the impetus for continuing.

Some would call the first group chickens the second hawks and the last eagles. I just believe that you have to have a passion for what you are doing, or you are in the wrong profession. You have to follow your heart to make a difference; that is the reward. That is the Eagle!

Sovereignty

The dictionary describes sovereignty in seven different applications. The one I am speaking about today is as a personal accomplishment. Therefore the definition is: "rightful status, independence or prerogative."

Over the last few months we have watched our sovereignty be questioned politically, financially, globally and probably individually as our abilities to maintain stability have been shaken.

We have witnessed and sometimes experienced family members or friends wonder how they will survive when so much of their once believed sovereignty has been washed away by the false security of the stock market and large corporations, to name a couple.

Whether you believe in bailouts or not is no longer the issue, it is done. What is important is how this affects you and your family. How do you reclaim what you once had and even assist it to grow so that a sovereign future can be yours, your children's, your employees?

We must retool our thinking and our actions. To do this we have to get outside of the traditional box, find the most affordable, stable and effective means of taking care of ourselves.

We must stop giving our decision making power to the old ways and embrace better and safer ways of guaranteeing the results that we are longing for.

We must grab the reigns of our future, trusting that we know what is best for us. Taking advantage of opportunities we may once have passed up. Take control of your future. You can do it and do it well.

Who Do We Serve? What is the Price?

Sometimes we are so busy *doing* our business that we can forget how and what it is that got us here.

When you visit Disneyland, or any other Disney location, you are never treated as a customer, but a guest. Every person who enters a Disney location is treated as the most perfect and important house guest. In fact, they are termed guests, not clients, customers or even visitors.

If you had someone whom you cherished visit your home, how would you treat them?

I know that we consider customers or clients differently because there it is a business deal. We also treat them differently because they are not in our personal space, but in our business space.

What would change in your business if each person were treated as an important guest and the red carpet (figuratively) were laid out for them in the same way as you would for your cherished guest at home?

I have, most recently, been privileged to be working with individuals whom I consider to have these qualities and they treat each person with such dignity that working with them has become an honor and a joy, never a JOB.

I have always attempted to treat others as I choose to be treated, yet with this experience I am learning even more about unconditional love and its expressions.

Breakthrough Techniques

What really is a breakthrough technique and how do you accomplish this in your organization?

Webster defines breakthrough in many ways. For our purpose it is a "sudden advance especially in knowledge or technique." Many times breakthroughs are referred to in medicine, however they take place in all industries.

For instance, here are some examples of breakthroughs.

Scientists have created 3D maps of the earth so small that a 1,000 of them could fit on one grain of sand. The breakthrough technique uses a tiny silicon tip with a sharp apex 100,000 times smaller than a sharpened pencil. This is a breakthrough in nanostructures.

In policing, experts have been able to detect corrosion from sweat on bullet, even if they are wiped clean. This was never possible before. This allows for convictions that may have remained as cold cases or unsolved mysteries.

A human rights breakthrough in Guatemala allows old documents, millions of pages stacked as high as your head, to be computerized and categorized in ways that once would have taken humans decades to accomplish. These documents reveal the truth from the Guatemalan Civil War from 1960-1996. Now the truth of the corruption and terrorism can be documented and perpetrators can be prosecuted. Some of the corrupt officials are still on the police force or within the military.

What are you doing within your organization to create breakthroughs to empower your people, maximize their potential and harness their creativity?

How do you create a breakthrough in the way that you "do business" to make it more cost effective and profitable in these stressful economic times?

I just wonder; how surprised you will be at your own discoveries?

Techniques for Your Safety

1. Increase your effort; lock steering columns, have tamper proof packaging; place packages in the trunk or cover them.

2. Carry your cell phone when away from home, control access to your business in appropriate ways. Have electronic tags to reduce theft.

3. When going out at night, go in groups of at least two. Leave signs of occupancy at home so people think that you are there. Support whistle blowers, they may save your life one day.

4. When parking at an off street location, be sure to utilize as much lighting as possible and check the front and back seats before you open the car to get in. Carry a flashlight.

5. Reduce the rewards for the thieves. Remember to take your wallet and keys with you. Use pre-paid phone cards for the holidays to avoid theft.

6. Monitor your children's comings and goings. Know where they are going and it's OK to have them contact you when they arrive.

7. Set rules for employees and managers to avoid harassment and/or short tempers. Always check ID's on Credit Cards.

8. Control public restrooms.

9. Consider alcohol free events for your holiday employee parties.

The Meaning of Peace
~Author Unknown

There was once a king who offered a prize to the artist who could paint the best picture of peace. Many artists tried. The king looked at all the pictures, but there were only two that he really liked, and he had to choose between them.

One picture was of a calm lake. The lake was a perfect mirror for the peaceful towering mountains all around it. Overhead was a blue sky with fluffy white clouds. All who saw this picture thought that it was a perfect picture of peace.

The second picture had mountains, too. But these were rugged and bare. Above was an angry sky from which rain fell, and in which lightening played.

Down the side of the mountain tumbled a foaming waterfall. This did not look peaceful at all.

But when the king looked, he saw behind the waterfall a tiny bush growing in a crack in the rock. In the bush a mother bird had built her nest.... a perfect picture of peace.

Which of the pictures won the prize?
The king chose the second picture.
Do you know why?

"Because," explained the king, "peace does not mean to be in a place where there is no noise, trouble or hard work. Peace means to be in the midst of all those things and still be calm in your heart. That is the real meaning of peace."

Tomb of The Unknown Soldier
Taken from the internet

Interesting facts about the Tomb of the Unknown Soldier and the Sentinels of the Third United States Infantry Regiment "Old Guard"

Q: How many steps does the guard take during his walk across the tomb of the Unknowns and why?

A: 21 steps. It alludes to the twenty-one gun salute, which is the highest honor given any military or foreign dignitary.

Q: How long does he hesitate after his about face to begin his return walk and why?

A: 21 seconds, for the same reason as answer number 1.

Q: Why are his gloves wet?

A: His gloves are moistened to prevent his losing his grip on the rifle.

Q: Does he carry his rifle on the same shoulder all the time, and if not, why not?

A: No, he carries the rifle on the shoulder away from the tomb. After his march across the path, he executes an about face and moves the rifle to the outside shoulder.

Q: How often are the guards changed?

A: Guards are changed every thirty minutes, twenty-four hours a day, 365 days a year.

Q: What are the physical traits of the guard limited to?

A: For a person to apply for guard duty at the tomb; he must be between 5' 10" and 6' 2" tall and his waist size cannot exceed 30".

Other requirements of the Guard:
Taken from the internet

They must commit 2 years of life to guard the tomb, live in a barracks under the tomb, and cannot drink any alcohol on or off duty FOR THE REST OF THEIR LIVES. They cannot swear in public FOR THE REST OF THEIR LIVES and cannot disgrace the uniform (fighting) or the tomb in any way.

After TWO YEARS, the guard is given a wreath pin that is worn on their lapel signifying they served as guard of the tomb. There are only 400 presently worn. The guard must obey these rules for the rest of their lives or give up the wreath pin.

The shoes are specially made with very thick soles to keep the heat and cold from their feet. There are metal heel plates that extend to the top of the shoe in order to make the loud click as they come to a halt. There are no wrinkles, folds or lint on the uniform. Guards dress for duty in front of a full-length mirror.

God Bless Our Troops and Their Families!

Generating Passive Income...Don't Let the Well Run Dry!

Have you ever wondered what you might do to keep the financial well pumped, especially in this kind of economy? What would you do to keep your family in your home, food on the table, and gas in your vehicle?

It can be easier than ever to generate a passive income if you just know how to do it. There are thousands of internet ideas, yet only a few have become financially wealthy. Another is the network marketing business, this too, has its drawbacks as it seems you must get in on the ground floor to really benefit.

Let's pose some interesting questions before you jump into something out of an emotional frenzy or the fear that stems from the "something is better than nothing syndrome." Let's spend a few moments creating your next step now so that your well never has to run dry.

Here are some introductory questions that you may choose to ponder:
1.) What is my passion and what do I know a lot about?
2.) If I do this, is it going to bring me joy, much like a hobby that pays for itself?
3.) Am I going to love it for the long haul?
4.) What resources do I have and or need to make this successful?
5.) How much time will it take to make this successful?
6.) Do I want to spend the upfront time it will take to make this profitable?
7.) What do I need to know about this endeavor's history and its possibilities?
8.) How much am I willing to commit to this to keep it running smoothly?
9.) What is the ROI (return on investment) and how long will it take to be profitable?
10.) Does the market need this? Want this? If so why?
11.) Do I have someone in my corner who can answer my "get started" questions?

Four Solutions for Resolving Conflict

Here are four steps that you can take to alter difficult behavior and move into some common ground.

These four steps can be used whether in resolving personal relationships or in business situations.

1. Create a physical space to get connected with your feelings and with the other party. You must do this to actually "be in the game."

2. Own your feelings. Once you have the space and you are connected, own how you feel. No one can refute your feelings, just your behaviors. Only you know how you feel and it is your feelings that connect you to the situation.

3. Make a decision to release the "it" that got you where you are. Revealed truth helps us to evaluate and discover the wisdom of releasing your "it."

4. Release the negativity and stress of "it." Ideal results can happen when you can release the negativity and the worry. It takes determined action to bring about these results.

These are steps that each of can take to make our lives and workplace what we choose them to be. I have been using these steps in mediations and business conflicts for over 20 years.

Let Freedom Ring!

How appropriate for this celebration of Martin Luther King, Jr. and his Dream for America and the world.

We watch with trepidation as civilians in Egypt, Libya, Syria and beyond, all fight for what they believe freedom to be.

Yet, how many of us really know freedom? We have been held hostage by the banking system, the mortgage rates and Wall Street for so many decades that the idea of freedom is all we have.

Yes, we live in the greatest country in the world and we have gotten as close to freedom as any country on this planet, yet none of us have ever lived in real freedom, nor do we know what it is or how to act if we had it.

I believe that to live in real freedom we must honor all view points with non-judgment.

To live in real freedom we must love one another without judgment of lifestyle, religious affiliation or political association. I have never met anyone, including me who is that free.

We must also allow viewpoints and attitudes that are 180° apart from ours to exist.

I think that Martin Luther King, Jr was on his way to some of this and I just wonder when we will actually take the next step and make a real difference.

When will we really take care of each other in ways that offer the freedom of unconditional love and living to each person, no matter what?

I just wonder.

Eight Ways People Drive You Crazy at Work!

You know what I am talking about; the gum chewer who loves to pop their gum. The girl at the desk next to yours who uses enough perfume for it to be considered a "clean air" spray or the one down the hall who is the incessant talker. We all know these people and have run into them somewhere along the line; maybe we even work with one of them now!

However, the issues that have come to my attention are a little different, not that those mentioned don't rank right up there with high levels of annoyance.

Here is a list of just a few.

1. Know your telephone etiquette; there is nothing that will lose a client faster than poor telephone skills.

2. The incessant "hoverer;" those who love to help by hovering right over you at your desk. Can you even *think* when this happens?

3. Gossip and Drama! Keep it to yourself. If someone is having difficulties with another, ask them to politely speak to that person about it, and then let them know that it is really none of your business.

4. Micro-managing; need I say more?

5. Interrupters: When you are on the phone and the person just bounces into your office, plops down and becomes an eavesdropper on your entire conversation. *Really!*

6. Favoritism: This is really disrespectful to all employees and even worse when it is perpetuated from the top or close to the top.

7. The Complainer: These are the ones who don't do a "good job," yet love to complain about their situation.

8. Late Comers: These are the *"always late to meetings people."* They are disrespectful of everyone else who showed up on time.

They Say, Take a Break….. *Really?*

I can hear you already. I don't have time to take a bathroom break much less "just a break!"

I understand. What if I told you that taking a fifteen minute or even ten minute break and going for a walk right outside to smell the fresh air or get some sunlight would increase your work results positively?

Taking a short break has the benefits of:

1. Increasing your work productivity for the day

2. Allowing you to focus or refocus on the issues at hand

3. Putting a smile on your face where it might have been a frown!

4. It might just lower your blood pressure for a time; just a thought!

5. Providing clarity where confusion used to reside.

6. Re-energizing the body and mind better than a candy bar or soda.
   (At least with fewer calories and sugar.)

These are just a few ideas to relieve tension for you that, if you are like me or many others I know, resides at the back of your neck and can easily cause a headache that even aspirin won't cure.

However you decide to reduce your tension, refocus and provide clarity for yourself, taking a break for five to ten minutes surely has to be one of the easiest, least expensive and most productive ways to do it.

Leader or Manager? You Decide

What does Webster's Dictionary have to say about leadership? Leadership is defined as, *"being one who demonstrates guides or provides a directing hand, one who is in the forefront."*

Managing and leading have two distinctly different functions. One is much more of a position of control while the latter is much gentler, more allowing, and more empowering. A true leader teaches by example, not control.

If you notice the feeling states around each of these, you might notice that management feels more closed, tight and darker. Therefore these sensations can be described as meaning that there is less light around the activity of managing. Additionally it feels like there is less breathing space. It can leave you with a feeling of being choked off or stopped in some way.

There is an actual mental space for creativity to take place when leadership is evoked. Leadership engenders just the opposite within your body. There is more space. You can breathe more freely. You do not feel stopped, left behind, or left out. The creative centers within you open wide, like a fresh breeze on a warm summer day. Which do you prefer?

Consider for a moment what you believe about yourself. Are you a good manager, directing people to do what you require of them? Or do you focus on inspiring others to do their best, gaining a result that, quite possibly, is better than the original desired outcome. I just wonder.

Help Stop Abuse!

In today's economy and with the level of chaos all over the world, it can be beneficial to understand some of the facts regarding violence within our environments. Please, remember that if it happens at work; it is happening at home as well. We all need to treat each other with more love and compassion. We need greater understanding.

We must first consider that violence is not always "Going Postal" as is the expression. Violence also includes harassment, physically, emotionally, mentally and sexually.

These types of violence can and often do escalate into more violent types of behavior. The financial costs to businesses have skyrocketed and are well into the billions of dollars ($13.5 at last count.) Over 500,000 employees miss over 1,750,000 work days per year and there is a 41% increase in stress levels; one in four workers is attacked each year. These are not the most recent figures.

We must know what to look for and as a business leader, manager or director; you must have a plan in place to deal with these issues. We must offer assistance in many forms.

Signs of a potentially violent person include:
1. A loner; one who is withdrawn, is afraid of change and feels no one listens to him/her.
2. Emotional problems; low self-esteem, depression, substance abuse; antagonistic relationships with others.
3. Career frustration; i.e. migratory job history or significant tenure on the same job. Also job loss after many years, company cut backs.
4. Obsessions; e.g. weapons, romantic/sexual, political or religious zealot, serious obsessive compulsive behavior.

The greatest myth is "it won't happen to you." Please have a plan in place to assist these people and deal with issues before they take place; 85% of the people exhibit clear warning signs before acting out. Please, Stay Safe.

Bringing Your Heritage into the Present

Here are some lessons to live by and to remember in these chaotic days. Whether it is the strange weather patterns, the financial crisis that this nation and the world are living through or simply the day to day stress of work and family; here are some qualities that we can all bring into our lives and our future.

PASSION: it is easy to attract people to the cause.

FOCUS: on what is important. Deciding what those important things are and not deviating, yet staying flexible. Waste no time on the foolish and undeliverable.

HUMILITY: Leaders are usually quiet and willing to take the blame while passing on the credits

RISK TAKERS: Breaking the rules in service to others. Taking Risks that break the rules in service of the heart

THREE GOALS: These are the critical goals that will move you forward and continue to create new possibilities along the way. Once you choose these goals, do not deviate from them. Just three for the year, please.

ATTENTION TO DETAIL: The difference between the gold and the silver can be one $1/100^{th}$ of a second.

RIGHT ALIGNMENT: Placing the correct people in place to match your vision. Right people, right spot, right discrimination.

CREATIVITY: It takes the creative resources of an entire tribe or organization to inspire new ideas. Always value your employees; they are the heart of your community or government.

INTEGRITY: Provide employment that embraces tribal values and translating those values into a lifetime of loyalty.

Decision Making Tips

One thing that I have learned over the course of my life is to always trust myself. So many times in the past when I was making difficult decisions or ones that cost me; *(physically, mentally, emotionally or financially)* I relied on the thoughts or feelings of someone else. Yet in the long run, it was my life or business that was impacted by the decision.

Each time there is an important decision to be made I <u>always</u> have a feeling or an inner nudge to direct me in the most positive way. The problem — for many of us — is that fear gets in the way. "What if" are powerful words and unfortunately we ask ourselves, *"what if it does not work?"* instead of *"**What if it DOES?**"*

Four Tips to Assist:

#1. Do not shush your inner voice. It is <u>always</u> right!

#2. When seeking advice; always go to someone with greater knowledge in that area than you have and who offers positive, constructive advice; advice that is in your best interest.

#3. Get clear mentally and emotionally before making any important decision. Always make your decision logically. You can add the emotions after it works!

#4. When dealing with employees; ask yourself, is this decision True? Is it Kind? Is it Necessary? Even in business, the decisions we make regarding people serve us best when these questions are answered from this positive viewpoint. *(Sometimes the kindest is not the easiest. Letting someone go, as an example, can at times meet these criterion.)*

What is Your Courage Potential?

What are some of the times and places where courage would be an advantage to you within your workplace?

~ What about when there is a customer/client who is rude and rather unsavory and you really choose to politely let them know that this type of behavior is not appreciated or allowed. You must do this without alienating them forever.

~ What about when the boss asks you to do something that you know to be detrimental to the organization, the team or an individual? Perhaps it is even illegal!

~ What is your courage potential when you see another employee – or even the boss – bullying one of your co-workers?

You don't have to be "Brave Heart" to stand up for yourself or for others, yet standing up and being courageous can be difficult.

Instead of standing by the wayside and condemning this behavior out of fear of reprisal, you can speak to the person who is behaving in an unacceptable manner in a calm and positive voice. Share with him/her out of a real concern for them; after all, the core feelings behind all of these behaviors is FEAR.

Fear can be a destroyer of relationships and business, yet it is really a "NO THING." Fear only exists when there is an unwarranted belief that something might go wrong. Fear takes over when doubt creeps in. Doubt creeps in when we stop believing in ourselves and give up.

You already know the ways to behave in these circumstances, you simply need to believe in yourself and know that truth and love do prevail!

Remember, 98% of Our Fars NEVER Come True!
So how much of your life are you wasting in fear?

Taking a Mental Health Break

Taking a mental health break doesn't always mean taking a full day or more to feel better. Many times one just needs to get up, walk around the area for a few minutes or when there is nice weather, just take a short walk outside. You don't have to go far, but taking a short 10-15 minute mental health break can lower blood pressure, relax the body and mind and even change your mood to one of acceptance, instead of, &^%&^%&*^*&^; well, you fill in the blank depending on your style.

Much of the time we are worried about what our external clients/customers feel about our work or service that we forget to consider our internal customers.

You know who I mean. The people who work just down the hall or across the complex. Those who serve us in different ways; taxes, accounting, delivery, dispatch, administration services, second or third shifts and the list goes on.

Why is it only "me" who does my job correctly and everyone else has diminished capacity in some way or another? If only "they" would pay attention to what "I" need, they would be so much better at their job! *REALLY?*

Perhaps it is when we begin to believe that we are more important, that our needs are more critical than anyone else's, it is time for a mental health break. I'm just saying.

Now it is time to take that walk, play that computer game for five minutes, put yourself in their shoes and view the world from their perspective or say a kind word. BREATHE! Close your office door if you have one, and take a few minutes to reclaim your sanity. It can make a huge difference in how we treat ourselves and clearly how we treat others.

Remember, one smile can affect 1500 people. Who are you affecting today? And How?

"You Said to Lean on Your Arm…
And I Am Leaning.

You Said to Trust in Your Love…
And I Am Trusting.

You Said to Call on Your Name…
And I Am Calling.

I Am Stepping Out
on Your Word."
~ **Dr. Maya Angelo**

Photographer unknown